contents

Please note that Australian cup and
spoon measurements are metric.
A conversion chart appears on page 62.

salmon, avocado and dill salad

500g frozen broad beans
200g baby spinach leaves
2 trimmed celery stalks
(200g), sliced thinly
2 medium avocados,
peeled, sliced
1½ cups (375ml) water
1½ cups (375ml) fish stock
½ cup (125ml) dry white wine
4 dill stalks
6 whole black peppercorns
1 clove garlic, halved
500g skinless salmon fillets
dill and mustard dressing
1 clove garlic, crushed
½ cup (125ml) olive oil
¼ cup (60ml) white wine
vinegar
2 teaspoons dijon mustard
1 teaspoon finely chopped
fresh dill

Boil, steam or microwave beans until just tender; drain, remove and discard the outer shells. Combine beans, spinach, celery and avocado in large bowl.

Make dill and mustard dressing.

Combine the water, stock, wine, dill, peppercorns and garlic in large shallow frying pan. Bring to a gentle simmer.

Add salmon to pan and simmer gently, uncovered, about 5 minutes or until cooked as desired, turning salmon over halfway through cooking.

Drain salmon from pan, transfer to plate. Using two forks, flake salmon into large pieces. Gently toss salmon with bean mixture and half of the dill and mustard dressing.

Serve salad drizzled with remaining dressing.

Dill and mustard dressing Place ingredients in screw-top jar; shake well.

serves 4
per serving 54g fat; 2925kJ (699 cal)

smoked chicken salad

Smoked chicken has already been cooked during the curing process, making this a simple salad to throw together at short notice. You can keep a smoked chicken in your freezer; just thaw it before slicing.

400g smoked chicken breast
200g baby spinach leaves
1 medium yellow capsicum (200g), sliced thinly
1 medium red onion (170g), sliced thinly
1 cup firmly packed fresh purple basil leaves
2 teaspoons finely grated lime rind
¼ cup (60ml) lime juice
2 tablespoons coarsely chopped fresh coriander
2 small fresh red thai chillies, seeded, chopped finely
2 teaspoons peanut oil
1 teaspoon sugar

Remove and discard any skin from chicken; slice chicken thinly.
Combine chicken, spinach, capsicum, onion and basil in large bowl.
Combine remaining ingredients in screw-top jar; shake well.
Pour dressing over salad; toss gently to combine.

serves 4
per serving 13.9g fat; 998kJ (238 cal)

beef and rice salad

2 tablespoons plum sauce
1 tablespoon kecap manis
1 teaspoon sesame oil
400g beef eye fillet
2 cups (400g) white
 medium-grain rice
2½ cups (625ml) water
150g sugar snap peas,
 trimmed
130g can corn kernels,
 rinsed, drained
100g baby spinach leaves
4 green onions, sliced thinly
chilli soy dressing
1 clove garlic, crushed
2 small fresh red thai
 chillies, sliced
⅓ cup (80ml) soy sauce
2 tablespoons peanut oil
2 teaspoons sesame oil

Combine sauce, kecap manis and oil in medium bowl. Add beef and stir well; cover, refrigerate 3 hours or overnight.

Preheat oven to moderately hot.

Combine rice and the water in large saucepan, bring to a boil, stirring occasionally. Lower heat, cover; simmer 10 minutes. Remove from heat; stand, covered, 5 minutes.

Meanwhile, heat oiled flameproof baking dish over medium-high heat, add beef; cook until browned all over. Transfer dish to moderately hot oven; roast about 25 minutes or until beef is cooked as desired. Stand 10 minutes before slicing thinly.

Meanwhile, boil, steam or microwave peas until just tender.

Make chilli soy dressing.

Combine rice, peas, corn, spinach, onion and dressing in large bowl; toss gently. Serve topped with beef.

Chilli soy dressing Combine ingredients in screw-top jar; shake well.

serves 4
per serving 17.7g fat; 2755kJ (658 cal)

roasted pumpkin, sesame and rocket salad

You will need a piece of pumpkin weighing approximately 750g for this recipe; we used butternut, but you can use whatever pumpkin variety you like.

600g trimmed pumpkin
cooking-oil spray
1 tablespoon honey
1 tablespoon sesame seeds
500g asparagus, halved
150g baby rocket leaves
1 small red onion (100g), sliced thinly
1 tablespoon sesame oil
1 tablespoon cider vinegar
1 teaspoon honey, extra

Preheat oven to very hot.
Cut pumpkin into 1.5cm wide strips.
Place pumpkin, in single layer, in baking-paper-lined dish; spray lightly with cooking-oil spray. Roast, uncovered, in very hot oven about 20 minutes or until pumpkin is just tender. Drizzle with honey; sprinkle with seeds. Roast 5 minutes, uncovered, or until seeds are browned lightly.
Meanwhile, boil, steam or microwave asparagus until just tender; drain. Rinse under cold water; drain.
Combine pumpkin, asparagus, rocket and onion in large bowl. Drizzle with combined remaining ingredients; toss salad gently.

serves 4
per serving 7.2g fat; 744kJ (178 cal)
tip Reserve any seeds or honey from the pumpkin pan and add to the dressing.

egg, potato and spinach salad

8 kipfler or tiny new potatoes
6 eggs
4 bacon rashers, sliced thickly
100g baby spinach leaves
¼ cup coarsely chopped fresh chives
60g parmesan cheese, shaved
mustard dressing
2 tablespoons olive oil
1 tablespoon red wine vinegar
2 teaspoons wholegrain mustard

Boil, steam or microwave potatoes until tender; drain. Slice potatoes thickly.

Place eggs in small saucepan, cover with cold water. Bring to a boil, stirring (this will centre the yolks), then simmer, uncovered, 5 minutes. Drain, cover with cold water, then remove the shells. Quarter eggs lengthways.

Cook bacon in large frying pan until crisp; drain on absorbent paper.

Make mustard dressing.

Combine spinach, potato, bacon, chives and mustard dressing in large bowl; toss gently. Divide among serving plates, add egg and parmesan flakes.

Mustard dressing Combine ingredients in screw-top jar; shake well.

serves 4
per serving 21.9g fat; 1414kJ (337 cal)

crispy noodle salad

Crispy fried noodles are sold packaged (usually in a 100g packet), already deep-fried and ready to eat. They are sometimes labelled crunchy noodles, and are available in two widths – thin and spaghetti-like, or wide and flat, like fettuccine. We used the thin variety in this recipe.

1 medium red capsicum (200g)
100g baby curly endive
100g crispy fried noodles
1 small red onion (100g), sliced thinly
1 tablespoon coarsely chopped fresh mint
1 tablespoon coarsely chopped fresh coriander
dressing
⅓ cup (80ml) peanut oil
1 tablespoon white vinegar
1 tablespoon brown sugar
1 tablespoon light soy sauce
1 teaspoon sesame oil
1 clove garlic, crushed

Cut capsicum in half lengthways. Remove and discard seeds and membranes; slice capsicum pieces thinly. Trim endive; discard hard ends of leaves.
Combine capsicum and endive with noodles, onion and herbs in large bowl. Add dressing; toss to combine.
Dressing Combine ingredients in screw-top jar; shake well.

serves 4
per serving 22.7g fat; 1104kJ (264 cal)

chilli lime chicken salad

1½ cups (375ml) chicken stock
1½ cups (375ml) water
4 single chicken breast fillets (680g)
1 small red capsicum (150g), sliced thinly
6 radishes, sliced thinly
½ large chinese cabbage (300g), shredded thickly
3 green onions, sliced
1 cup (80g) bean sprouts
½ cup loosely packed coriander leaves
½ cup (75g) salted peanuts, toasted
dressing
⅓ cup (80ml) lime juice
¼ cup (65g) grated palm sugar or brown sugar
2 small fresh red thai chillies, chopped finely
1 clove garlic, crushed
1 tablespoon fish sauce
¼ cup (60ml) olive oil

Bring stock and the water to a boil in large
frying pan. Add chicken; simmer gently, uncovered,
about 8 minutes, turning halfway, or until just cooked
through. Remove from heat; cool chicken in liquid.
Meanwhile, make dressing.
Cut chicken into thin slices.
Combine remaining ingredients in large bowl.
Add half of the dressing and gently toss until
combined. Serve chicken on salad and drizzle
with remaining dressing.
Dressing Combine juice, sugar, chilli and garlic
in small saucepan. Stir over low heat until sugar
is dissolved. Cool and whisk in sauce and olive oil
until combined.

serves 4
per serving 28g fat; 2210kJ (528 cal)

watercress salad with cheese balls

We used corella pears for this recipe. You will need a bunch of watercress weighing about 350g in total to yield the leaves required for this salad.

3 small pears (540g), sliced thinly
1 teaspoon finely grated orange rind
½ cup (125ml) orange juice
300g snow peas, trimmed
100g watercress leaves
cheese balls
150g ricotta cheese
100g fetta cheese
¼ cup (30g) finely grated cheddar cheese
1 tablespoon finely chopped fresh flat-leaf parsley
1 tablespoon finely chopped fresh chives
2 teaspoons finely chopped fresh thyme
1 teaspoon curry powder
1 teaspoon sweet paprika

Combine pear, rind and juice in large bowl. Cover; refrigerate 15 minutes.
Meanwhile, boil, steam or microwave snow peas until just tender; drain. Rinse under cold water; drain.
Gently toss pear mixture, snow peas and watercress in large bowl. Serve topped with cheese balls.
Cheese balls Combine cheeses and herbs in small bowl. Roll level teaspoons of mixture into balls. Combine curry powder and paprika in small bowl; gently toss half of the cheese balls in curry mixture until coated.

serves 4
per serving 13g fat; 1070kJ (256 cal)

zucchini, eggplant and bean salad

3 medium zucchini (360g)
2 medium eggplants (600g)
4 medium egg tomatoes (600g)
1 tablespoon cumin seeds
½ cup (125ml) extra virgin olive oil
⅓ cup (80ml) lemon juice
2 cloves garlic, crushed
½ teaspoon freshly ground black pepper
2 x 400g cans cannellini beans, rinsed, drained
½ cup firmly packed fresh coriander leaves

Cut zucchini lengthways into 5mm slices.
Cut eggplant into 5mm rounds.
Cook eggplant and zucchini in heated oiled grill pan (or grill or barbecue) until browned on both sides and tender.
Cut tomatoes into quarters, remove seeds and chop flesh coarsely.
Add cumin seeds to heated dry frying pan; cook, stirring, until seeds are fragrant and begin to pop.
Combine oil, juice, garlic, pepper and cumin seeds in screw-top jar; shake well.
Combine beans, zucchini, eggplant and tomato in large bowl, stir in oil mixture and coriander leaves.

serves 6
per serving 20g fat; 1145kJ (274 cal)

curried lamb and lentil salad

2 tablespoons mild curry paste
¼ cup (60ml) olive oil
600g lamb sirloin (or eye of loin or backstrap)
1 medium brown onion (150g), chopped
1 large carrot (180g), chopped
1 trimmed celery stalk (100g), chopped
1 clove garlic, crushed
⅓ cup (80ml) chicken stock
400g can brown lentils, rinsed, drained
100g baby spinach leaves
½ cup loosely packed fresh coriander leaves

Combine 1 tablespoon of the curry paste and
1 tablespoon of the oil in small bowl. Rub lamb
with curry mixture.
Cook lamb in heated oiled grill pan (or pan-fry) until
browned on both sides and cooked as desired.
Transfer to plate, cover; stand 5 minutes.
Meanwhile, heat remaining oil in medium frying pan.
Add onion, carrot and celery; cook, stirring, until
vegetables are softened. Add garlic and remaining
curry paste; cook, stirring, until fragrant. Add stock
and lentils, stir until hot. Remove from heat, add
spinach and coriander; toss until combined.
Serve lamb sliced with lentil salad.

serves 4
per serving 23.1g fat; 1739kJ (415 cal)

avocado caesar salad

2 small white bread rolls (80g), sliced thinly
1 clove garlic, crushed
1 tablespoon olive oil
2 baby cos lettuce
1 medium red onion (170g), sliced thinly
2 medium avocados (500g), chopped coarsely
⅓ cup (50g) sun-dried tomatoes in oil,
    drained, sliced thinly
60g parmesan cheese, shaved
dressing
1 clove garlic, crushed
2 egg yolks
2 teaspoons dijon mustard
2 tablespoons white vinegar
¾ cup (180ml) extra light olive oil
1 tablespoon water, approximately

Preheat oven to moderately hot.
Place bread slices, in single layer, on oven tray;
brush with combined garlic and oil. Toast in
moderately hot oven about 5 minutes or until crisp.
Meanwhile, make dressing.
Combine toast in large bowl with remaining
ingredients and dressing; toss gently to combine.
Dressing Blend or process garlic, yolks, mustard
and vinegar until smooth. With motor operating,
gradually add oil in a thin steady stream; process
until mixture thickens. Add enough water,
if desired, to make pouring consistency.

serves 4
per serving 75.2g fat; 3364kJ (804 cal)
tip The garlic toasts can be made a day ahead;
store in an airtight container.

tandoori chicken salad with pappadums

Pappadums are sun-dried crispbreads made from a combination of lentil and rice flours, oil and spices.

750g chicken tenderloins
¾ cup (200g) yogurt
2 tablespoons tandoori paste
8 pappadums
200g mesclun
4 large egg tomatoes (360g), chopped coarsely
2 lebanese cucumbers (260g), seeded, sliced thinly
1 small red onion (100g), sliced thinly
dressing
¼ cup (60ml) vegetable oil
¼ cup (60ml) lime juice
2 tablespoons hot mango chutney

Combine chicken, yogurt and paste in large bowl; toss to coat chicken in tandoori mixture.
Cook chicken, in batches, on heated oiled grill plate (or grill or barbecue), until browned all over and cooked through. Stand 5 minutes; slice thickly.
Meanwhile, place 2 pappadums on edge of microwave-safe plate. Cook on HIGH (100%) about 30 seconds or until puffed; repeat with remaining pappadums.
Combine chicken in large bowl with mesclun, tomato, cucumber, onion and dressing; toss gently. Serve salad with pappadums.
Dressing Combine ingredients in screw-top jar; shake well.

serves 4
per serving 28g fat; 2193kJ (525 cal)

honey soy chicken salad

You need about a quarter of a small savoy cabbage for this recipe.

600g chicken breast fillets,
   sliced thinly
2 tablespoons soy sauce
⅓ cup (115g) honey
1 clove garlic, crushed
4 small fresh red thai chillies,
   seeded, chopped finely
300g snow peas
1 small carrot (120g)
1 tablespoon peanut oil
2 cups (160g) finely shredded
   savoy cabbage
1 medium yellow capsicum (200g),
   sliced thinly
1 medium red capsicum (200g),
   sliced thinly
1 lebanese cucumber (130g),
   seeded, sliced thinly
4 green onions, sliced thinly
½ cup loosely packed
   fresh mint leaves
2 tablespoons lime juice
2 teaspoons sesame oil

Place chicken in medium bowl with sauce, honey, garlic and half of the chilli; toss to coat chicken in chilli mixture. Cover; refrigerate until required.
Boil, steam or microwave snow peas until just tender; drain. Rinse immediately under cold water; drain. Using vegetable peeler, slice carrot into ribbons.
Heat peanut oil in wok or large frying pan; stir-fry drained chicken, in batches, until browned and cooked through.
Place chicken, snow peas and carrot in large serving bowl with remaining ingredients and remaining chilli; toss gently to combine.

serves 4
per serving 15.8g fat; 1778kJ (425 cal)
tip You can use a large barbecued chicken instead of the breast fillets, if you prefer; discard bones and skin, then shred meat coarsely before tossing with remaining salad ingredients.

chicken, witlof and cashew salad

Like mushrooms, witlof is grown in the dark to retain its pale colour. Sometimes spelled witloof, and in some places known as belgian endive or chicory, this versatile and bittersweet vegetable is as good eaten cooked as it is raw. You need to purchase a large barbecued chicken, weighing approximately 900g, for this recipe.

1 medium witlof (175g)
2 baby cos lettuce
1 medium yellow capsicum (200g), sliced thinly
1 small red onion (100g), sliced thinly
1 cup (150g) roasted unsalted cashews
4 cups (400g) shredded chicken
dressing
1 cup (280g) yogurt
2 cloves garlic, crushed
2 teaspoons finely grated lemon rind
¼ cup (60ml) lemon juice
¼ cup loosely packed, coarsely chopped
   fresh coriander

Trim and discard 1cm from witlof base; separate leaves. Trim core from lettuce; separate leaves.
Place witlof and lettuce in large bowl with capsicum, onion, cashews, chicken and dressing; toss gently to combine.
Dressing Combine ingredients in screw-top jar; shake well.

serves 4
per serving 26.3g fat; 1737kJ (416 cal)
tip Roast the cashews briefly to bring out their flavour – in a small dry heavy-based frying pan, stirring, over medium heat.

chickpea salad

1½ cups (300g) dried chickpeas
250g cherry tomatoes, halved
1 large green cucumber (400g), seeded,
    chopped coarsely
1 medium red onion (170g), chopped finely
¼ cup finely shredded fresh mint leaves
¼ cup (60ml) lime juice
¼ cup (60ml) olive oil
2 teaspoons dijon mustard
¼ teaspoon sugar
2 cloves garlic, crushed

Place chickpeas in large bowl; cover with water.
Soak overnight; drain.
Cook chickpeas in large saucepan of boiling water,
uncovered, about 50 minutes or until tender; drain.
Rinse under cold water; drain.
Combine chickpeas in large bowl with tomato,
cucumber, onion and mint; toss gently with
combined remaining ingredients.

serves 8
per serving 9.2g fat; 743kJ (178 cal)
tips You can use canned rather than dried
chickpeas in this recipe. Rinse two 400g cans of
chickpeas well under cold water; drain thoroughly
before combining with other ingredients.
This recipe can be made a day ahead and
refrigerated, covered, overnight.

vegetable, haloumi and rocket salad

250g haloumi cheese, cut into 2cm cubes
180g button mushrooms, halved
1 medium red capsicum (200g), chopped coarsely
1 medium yellow capsicum (200g), chopped coarsely
3 baby eggplant (180g), chopped coarsely
2 medium zucchini (320g), sliced thickly
2 tablespoons olive oil
2 tablespoons balsamic vinegar
1 clove garlic, crushed
150g baby rocket leaves

Cook cheese, mushrooms, capsicums, eggplant and zucchini, in batches, on heated oiled grill plate (or grill or barbecue) until browned lightly and just tender.
Meanwhile, place oil, vinegar and garlic in screw-top jar; shake well.
Combine cheese and vegetables in large bowl with rocket and dressing; toss gently to combine.

serves 4
per serving 20.7g fat; 1229kJ (294 cal)

mediterranean chicken salad

1½ cups (375ml)
  chicken stock
½ cup (125ml) white wine
4 single chicken breast
  fillets (680g)
2 medium yellow
  capsicums (400g)
1 large loaf sourdough
  bread (500g)
100g butter, melted
2 cloves garlic, crushed
1 tablespoon finely chopped
  fresh flat-leaf parsley
200g baby rocket leaves
250g teardrop tomatoes,
  halved
⅓ cup (50g) black olives
anchovy dressing
½ cup firmly packed
  fresh basil leaves
½ cup (125ml) extra virgin
  olive oil
2 tablespoons finely grated
  parmesan cheese
2 drained anchovy fillets
1 tablespoon lemon juice

Preheat oven to very hot.

Combine stock and wine in medium frying pan, bring to a boil. Add chicken; simmer, loosely covered, about 8 minutes, turning halfway, until chicken is cooked through. Remove chicken from pan, stand 10 minutes before slicing.

Meanwhile, quarter capsicums, remove and discard seeds and membranes. Roast in very hot oven or under hot grill, skin side up, until skin blisters and blackens. Cover capsicum pieces with plastic or paper for 5 minutes; peel away skin, slice capsicum thinly.

Reduce oven temperature to moderately hot. Remove most of the crust from bread, cut into 1.5cm slices then cut into 3cm pieces. Divide bread pieces between two oven trays. Drizzle over combined melted butter, garlic and parsley then toss gently to coat bread pieces in butter mixture. Bake in moderately hot oven about 10 minutes or until browned lightly.

Meanwhile make anchovy dressing.

Arrange rocket, tomato, olives, chicken and capsicum on serving platter. Just before serving, toss through croutons and drizzle with anchovy dressing.

Anchovy dressing Blend ingredients until smooth.

serves 4
per serving 60.1g fat; 4506kJ (1076 cal)

green papaya salad

100g snake beans
850g green papaya
250g cherry tomatoes, quartered
3 small fresh green thai chillies, seeded,
   chopped finely
2 tablespoons finely chopped dried shrimp
¼ cup (60ml) lime juice
1 tablespoon fish sauce
1 tablespoon grated palm sugar or brown sugar
2 cloves garlic, crushed
¼ cup coarsely chopped fresh coriander
2 cups (120g) finely shredded iceberg lettuce
⅓ cup (50g) coarsely chopped roasted
   unsalted peanuts

Cut beans into 5cm pieces; cut pieces in half
lengthways. Boil, steam or microwave beans
until just tender; drain. Rinse immediately under
cold water; drain.
Meanwhile, peel papaya. Quarter lengthways,
remove seeds; grate papaya coarsely.
Place papaya and beans in large bowl with
tomato, chilli and shrimp. Add combined juice,
sauce, sugar, garlic and half of the coriander;
toss gently to combine.
Place lettuce on serving plates; spoon papaya
salad over lettuce, sprinkle with nuts and
remaining coriander.

serves 4
per serving 7g fat; 677kJ (162 cal)

asparagus and salmon pasta salad

*Shell pasta, or conchiglie, is available in three sizes.
In addition to the medium shell we used here, there is
a smaller shell called conchigliette, which makes a great
addition to soups, and a larger shell, called conchiglioni,
which is usually served stuffed and baked.*

375g shell pasta
400g asparagus, trimmed
415g can red salmon, drained, flaked
100g watercress, trimmed
1 small white onion (80g), sliced thinly
1 clove garlic, crushed
2 tablespoons wholegrain mustard
2 tablespoons red wine vinegar
2 tablespoons lemon juice
¼ cup (60ml) olive oil

Cook pasta in large saucepan of boiling water,
uncovered, until just tender; drain. Rinse under
cold water; drain.
Meanwhile, cut asparagus into 5cm lengths.
Boil, steam or microwave asparagus until just tender;
drain. Rinse under cold water; drain.
Combine pasta and asparagus in large bowl with
salmon, watercress and onion. Place remaining
ingredients in screw-top jar; shake well.
Drizzle dressing over pasta; toss gently to combine.

serves 4
per serving 25.2g fat; 2672kJ (638 cal)

beef salad with blue-cheese dressing

500g tiny new potatoes, quartered
1 tablespoon olive oil
4 beef fillet steaks (500g)
300g green beans, trimmed, halved crossways
200g grape tomatoes, halved
100g baby rocket leaves
blue-cheese dressing
¼ cup (60ml) olive oil
2 cloves garlic, crushed
¼ cup (60ml) orange juice
60g blue cheese, crumbled

Preheat oven to very hot.
Place potato, in single layer, in large shallow
baking dish; drizzle with oil. Roast, uncovered,
in very hot oven about 20 minutes or until lightly
browned and tender.
Meanwhile, make blue-cheese dressing.
Cook beef on heated oiled grill plate (or grill
or barbecue) until browned both sides and
cooked as desired. Cover; stand 5 minutes.
Meanwhile, boil, steam or microwave beans
until just tender; drain.
Slice beef thinly. Combine beef, beans and potato
in large bowl with tomato and rocket, drizzle with
blue-cheese dressing; toss gently to combine.
Blue-cheese dressing Combine ingredients
in screw-top jar; shake well.

serves 4
per serving 31.9g fat; 2143kJ (512 cal)

roast beef and rocket salad

1 tablespoon olive oil
600g piece beef eye fillet
500g tiny new potatoes, halved
120g semi-dried tomatoes
100g baby rocket leaves
1 small red onion (100g), sliced thinly
4 green onions, sliced thinly
½ cup (125ml) buttermilk
⅓ cup (100g) mayonnaise
1 tablespoon dijon mustard
1 clove garlic, crushed
1 teaspoon freshly ground black pepper

Preheat oven to moderately hot.
Heat oil in medium flameproof baking dish; cook
beef, turning, until browned. Roast, uncovered,
in moderately hot oven about 15 minutes or until
cooked as desired. Remove from oven. Cover;
stand 5 minutes, slice beef thinly.
Meanwhile, boil, steam or microwave potato
until just tender; drain.
Combine beef and potato in large bowl with
tomato, rocket and onions.
Combine remaining ingredients in screw-top jar;
shake well. Drizzle dressing over salad; toss
gently to combine.

serves 4
per serving 20.9g fat; 2095kJ (501 cal)
tip The beef can be cooked up to 2 hours ahead;
store, covered, in the refrigerator until required.

char-grilled beef salad

500g beef rump steak
¼ cup (60ml) fish sauce
¼ cup (60ml) lime juice
3 lebanese cucumbers (390g), seeded, sliced thinly
4 small fresh red thai chillies, sliced thinly
8 green onions, sliced thinly
250g cherry tomatoes, quartered
1 cup loosely packed vietnamese mint leaves
1 cup loosely packed coriander leaves
1 tablespoon grated palm sugar or brown sugar
2 teaspoons soy sauce
1 clove garlic, crushed

Combine beef with 2 tablespoons of the fish sauce and 1 tablespoon of the juice in large bowl; cover, refrigerate 3 hours or overnight.
Drain beef; discard marinade. Cook beef on heated oiled grill plate (or grill or barbecue) until browned both sides and cooked as desired. Cover, stand 5 minutes; slice thinly.
Meanwhile, combine cucumber, chilli, onion, tomato and herbs in large bowl.
Combine remaining juice and fish sauce with sugar, soy sauce and garlic in screw-top jar; shake well.
Add beef and dressing to salad; toss gently to combine.

serves 4
per serving 8.7g fat; 1008kJ (241 cal)

sesame chicken salad

You need to purchase a large barbecued chicken, weighing approximately 900g, for this recipe.

150g snow peas
4 cups (400g) shredded chicken
100g snow pea sprouts
2 cups (160g) bean sprouts
2 trimmed sticks celery (200g), sliced thinly
4 green onions, sliced thinly
1 tablespoon roasted sesame seeds
dressing
2 tablespoons peanut oil
2 teaspoons sesame oil
½ teaspoon five-spice powder
2 tablespoons kecap manis
1 tablespoon lime juice

Place snow peas in medium bowl. Cover with boiling water; drain immediately. Cover snow peas with cold water in same bowl; stand 2 minutes. Drain; slice thinly.
Combine snow peas in large bowl with chicken, snow pea sprouts, bean sprouts, celery, onion and dressing; toss gently to combine. Sprinkle with sesame seeds to serve.
Dressing Combine ingredients in screw-top jar; shake well.

serves 4
per serving 18.4g fat; 1188kJ (284 cal)
tip Sugar snap peas can also be used in this recipe.

spicy chicken salad

2 tablespoons long-grain
white rice
1 tablespoon peanut oil
1 tablespoon finely chopped
fresh lemon grass
2 small fresh red thai chillies,
seeded, chopped finely
2 cloves garlic, crushed
1 tablespoon finely chopped
fresh galangal
750g chicken mince
1 lebanese cucumber (130g),
seeded, sliced thinly
1 small red onion (100g),
sliced thinly
1¼ cups (100g)
bean sprouts
½ cup loosely packed fresh
thai basil leaves
1 cup loosely packed fresh
coriander leaves
4 large iceberg
lettuce leaves
dressing
⅓ cup (80ml) lime juice
2 tablespoons fish sauce
2 tablespoons kecap manis
2 tablespoons peanut oil
2 teaspoons grated palm
sugar or brown sugar
½ teaspoon sambal oelek

Heat dry wok; stir-fry rice until lightly browned.
Blend or process (or crush using mortar and
pestle) rice until it resembles fine breadcrumbs.
Heat oil in same wok; stir-fry lemon grass, chilli,
garlic and galangal until fragrant. Remove from
wok. Stir-fry chicken, in batches, until changed
in colour and cooked through.

Return chicken and lemon grass mixture to wok
with about a third of the dressing; stir-fry about
5 minutes or until mixture thickens slightly.

Place remaining dressing in large bowl with
chicken, cucumber, onion, sprouts and herbs;
toss gently to combine. Place lettuce leaves on
serving plates; divide chicken mixture among
leaves, sprinkle with ground rice.

Dressing Combine ingredients in screw-top jar;
shake well.

serves 4
per serving 29.7g fat; 1997kJ (477 cal)

char-grilled cuttlefish, rocket and parmesan salad

1kg cuttlefish hoods
1 tablespoon olive oil
1 tablespoon finely grated lemon rind
⅓ cup (80ml) lemon juice
1 clove garlic, crushed
150g rocket
150g semi-dried tomatoes, drained,
    chopped coarsely
1 small red onion (100g), sliced thinly
1 tablespoon drained baby capers, rinsed
80g parmesan cheese, shaved
2 tablespoons balsamic vinegar
⅓ cup (80ml) olive oil, extra

Halve cuttlefish lengthways, score insides in crosshatch pattern then cut into 5cm strips. Combine cuttlefish in medium bowl with oil, rind, juice and garlic, cover; refrigerate 10 minutes.
Meanwhile, combine rocket, tomato, onion, capers and cheese in large bowl.
Drain cuttlefish; discard marinade. Cook cuttlefish, in batches, on heated oiled grill plate (or grill or barbecue) until browned and cooked through.
Add cuttlefish to salad with combined vinegar and extra oil; toss gently to combine.

serves 4
per serving 34.3g fat; 2511kJ (600 cal)

merguez and couscous salad

*A small, spicy sausage – eaten throughout North Africa
and Spain – merguez is traditionally made with lamb
meat and is easily identified by its chilli-red colour.
Merguez can be found in many butchers, delicatessens
and sausage specialty stores, but any spicy sausage
can be used in this recipe.*

500g merguez sausages
1½ cups (375ml) beef stock
1½ cups (300g) couscous
20g butter
1 tablespoon finely grated lemon rind
¾ cup coarsely chopped fresh flat-leaf parsley
120g baby rocket leaves
⅓ cup (50g) toasted pine nuts
2 small fresh red thai chillies, seeded, sliced thinly
1 small red onion (100g), sliced thinly
1 clove garlic, crushed
⅓ cup (80ml) lemon juice
2 tablespoons olive oil

Cook sausages on heated grill plate (or grill or
barbecue) until browned and cooked through.
Drain on absorbent paper; slice thickly.
Meanwhile, bring stock to a boil in medium
saucepan. Remove from heat; stir in couscous and
butter. Cover; stand about 10 minutes or until liquid
is absorbed, fluffing couscous with fork occasionally.
Place sausage and couscous in large bowl with
remaining ingredients; toss gently to combine.

serves 4
per serving 45g fat; 3621kJ (865 cal)

chinese barbecued duck salad

Chinese barbecued duck is available from Asian grocery stores and specialty barbecued meat shops.

1 chinese barbecued duck
200g dried rice stick noodles
¾ cup loosely packed fresh coriander leaves
¾ cup loosely packed fresh mint leaves
2 lebanese cucumbers (260g), seeded, sliced thinly
½ cup (75g) toasted cashews
chilli lime dressing
2 large fresh green chillies, seeded, chopped finely
1 stalk fresh lemon grass, chopped finely
1 clove garlic, crushed
1 teaspoon coarsely grated lime rind
¼ cup (60ml) lime juice
2 tablespoons peanut oil
1 tablespoon brown sugar
1 tablespoon fish sauce
2 teaspoons sesame oil

Discard skin and bones from duck; chop duck meat coarsely.
Place noodles in medium heatproof bowl, cover with boiling water, stand until just tender; drain. Rinse under cold water; drain.
Meanwhile, make chilli lime dressing.
Combine duck and noodles in large bowl with herbs and cucumber, drizzle with dressing; toss gently to combine. Top with nuts before serving.
Chilli lime dressing Combine ingredients in screw-top jar; shake well.

serves 4
per serving 35g fat; 2712kJ (648 cal)

niçoise salad

The original French salade niçoise was created with the finest Provençale ingredients – vine-ripened tomatoes, local capers, hand-picked baby beans and fresh tuna caught just off the coast. Our version has adapted a modern approach, better suited to our hectic lifestyle.

200g baby green beans, trimmed
3 medium tomatoes (570g), cut into wedges
4 hard-boiled eggs, quartered
425g can tuna in springwater, drained, flaked
½ cup (80g) drained caperberries, rinsed
½ cup (60g) seeded small black olives
¼ cup firmly packed fresh flat-leaf parsley
440g can whole baby potatoes, rinsed,
    drained, halved
2 tablespoons olive oil
1 tablespoon lemon juice
2 tablespoons white wine vinegar

Boil, steam or microwave beans until just tender; drain. Rinse under cold water; drain.
Meanwhile, combine tomato, egg, tuna, caperberries, olives, parsley and potato in large bowl.
Combine remaining ingredients in screw-top jar; shake well. Add beans to salad, drizzle with dressing; toss gently to combine.

serves 4
per serving 17.8g fat; 1493kJ (357 cal)
tip This recipe is best made just before serving.

cold prawn and noodle salad

200g bean thread noodles
1 clove garlic, crushed
2 tablespoons fish sauce
1 tablespoon lime juice
2 teaspoons peanut oil
¼ cup (35g) coarsely chopped roasted
   unsalted peanuts
2 green onions, sliced thinly
¼ cup coarsely chopped fresh coriander
2 small fresh red thai chillies, seeded, sliced thinly
1kg large cooked king prawns, peeled, deveined

Place noodles in large heatproof bowl; cover with boiling water. Stand until just tender; drain. Using kitchen scissors, cut noodles into random lengths.
Whisk garlic, sauce, juice and oil in large bowl to combine.
Add noodles to bowl with nuts, onion, coriander, chilli and prawns; toss gently to combine.

serves 4
per serving 7.8g fat; 1353kJ (323 cal)

glossary

bacon rashers also known as bacon slices; made from cured and smoked pork side.

basil we use sweet basil, unless otherwise specified.
thai: also known as horapa, it has a slight licorice taste.

bean sprouts also known as bean shoots; tender new growths of assorted beans and seeds germinated for consumption as sprouts.

bean thread noodles also known as cellophane or glass noodles; white in colour, very delicate and fine, and available dried in various size bundles.

broad beans also known as fava, windsor and horse beans; available dried, fresh, canned and frozen. Peel twice when using fresh or frozen (discard outer long green pod and beige-green tough inner shell).

butter use salted or unsalted (sweet) butter; 125g is equal to one stick of butter.

buttermilk available from refrigerated dairy sections in supermarkets.

cannellini beans small, dried white bean. Sometimes sold as butter beans.

caperberries fruit formed after the caper buds have flowered; caperberries are pickled, usually with stalks intact.

capers the grey-green buds of a warm-climate shrub, sold either dried and salted or pickled in vinegar brine; tiny young ones, called baby capers, are also available.

capsicum also known as bell pepper or, simply, pepper; available in variety of colours. Discard membranes and seeds before use.

cheese
blue: mould-treated cheese mottled with blue veining.
fetta: a crumbly textured goat- or sheep-milk cheese with a sharp, salty taste.
haloumi: a firm, cream-coloured sheep-milk cheese matured in brine.
ricotta: soft, white, sweet cow-milk cheese with a slightly grainy texture.

chicken tenderloin thin strip of meat lying under the breast.

chickpeas also called channa, garbanzos or hummus; round, sandy-coloured legume.

chilli available in many different types and sizes. Use rubber gloves when seeding and chopping fresh chillies as they can burn your skin.

chinese barbecued duck has sweet-sticky coating made from soy sauce, sherry, hoisin sauce and five-spice; available from Asian food stores.

chinese cabbage also known as peking or napa cabbage, wong bok or petsai; elongated with pale-green crinkly leaves.

cos lettuce also known as romaine lettuce.

couscous fine, grain-like cereal product, made from semolina.

cumin seeds also known as zeera.

curly endive also known as frisee, a curly-leafed green vegetable.

curry paste some recipes in this book call for commercially prepared pastes of various strengths and flavours.

curry powder a blend of ground spices used for convenience when making Indian food.

eggplant also known as aubergine.

eggs some recipes in this book call for raw or barely cooked eggs; exercise caution if there is a salmonella problem in your area.

fish sauce also known as nam pla or nuoc nam. Made from pulverised, salted, fermented fish; has a pungent smell and strong taste.

five-spice powder a fragrant mixture of ground cinnamon, cloves, star anise, sichuan pepper and fennel seeds.

fried noodles crispy egg noodles packaged already deep-fried.

galangal also known as ka, a rhizome with hot ginger-citrusy flavour; used similarly to ginger and garlic as a seasoning and as an ingredient. Fresh ginger can be substituted for fresh galangal but the flavour of the dish will not be the same.

iceberg lettuce heavy, round lettuce with tightly packed leaves and crisp texture.

kecap manis thick, sweet soy sauce; depending on brand, the sweetness is derived from the addition of either molasses or palm sugar when brewed.

kipfler potato small, finger-shaped potato with a nutty flavour and creamy flesh.

lebanese cucumber also known as european or burpless cucumber; short and slender.

lemon grass a lemon-smelling and -tasting, sharp-edged grass; the white lower part of the stem is used in cooking.

lentils (red, brown, yellow) dried pulses often identified by and named after their colour.

mayonnaise we use whole-egg mayonnaise in our recipes.

merguez sausage a small, spicy sausage traditionally made with lamb meat.

mesclun salad mix of assorted young lettuce and other green leaves, including mizuna, baby spinach leaves, curly endive.

mince also known as ground meat, as in beef, pork, lamb and veal.

mustard
dijon: pale brown, distinctively flavoured, mild French mustard.
wholegrain: also known as seeded. French-style coarse-grain mustard made from crushed mustard seeds and dijon-style French mustard.

oil
peanut: pressed from ground peanuts; has high smoke point (capacity to handle high heat without burning).
sesame: made from white sesame seeds; a flavouring rather than a cooking medium.

onion
green: also known as scallion or (incorrectly) shallot; onion picked before bulb forms. Has long, bright-green edible stalk.
red: also known as spanish, red spanish or bermuda onion; large, sweet purple-red onion.

papaya, green available at Asian food stores; look for one that is hard and slightly shiny, proving it is freshly picked. Papaya will soften rapidly if not used within a day or two.

paprika ground, dried red capsicum (bell pepper); available sweet or hot.

pine nuts also known as pignoli; small, cream-coloured kernel from pine cones.

prawns also known as shrimp.

pumpkin also known as squash.

rice stick noodles, dried also known as sen lek, ho fun or kway teow; come in varying widths – all should be soaked in hot water until soft.

rocket also known as arugula, rugula and rucola; a peppery-tasting green leaf.

sambal oelek also ulek or olek; salty Indonesian paste made from chillies and vinegar.

savoy cabbage large, heavy head with crinkled dark-green outer leaves.

sesame seeds black and white are the most common of this small oval seed.

shrimp, dried also known as goong hang, salted sun-dried tiny prawns. They are sold packaged, shelled as a rule, in all Asian grocery stores.

snake beans long (about 40cm), thin, fresh green beans that are Asian in origin.

snow peas also called mange tout ("eat all").

soy sauce also known as sieu; made from fermented soy beans. We used a mild Japanese variety.

spinach also known as english spinach and incorrectly, silverbeet. Baby spinach leaves are used raw in salads.

stock 1 cup (250ml) stock is the equivalent of 1 cup (250ml) water plus 1 crumbled stock cube (or 1 teaspoon stock powder).

sugar snap peas also known as honey snap peas; fresh small peas which can be eaten whole, pod and all, similarly to snow peas.

sugar
brown: a soft, fine granulated sugar retaining molasses for its colour and flavour.
palm: also known as nam tan pip, jaggery, and jawa or gula melaka; made from the sap of the sugar palm tree. Use brown sugar as a substitute.

tandoori paste commercially packaged paste; available in supermarkets.

tomato
cherry: also known as tiny tim or tom thumb tomatoes.
egg: also called plum or roma; smallish and oval-shaped.
grape: small, slightly elongated tomato.
semi-dried: partially dried tomato pieces in olive oil. Not a preserve so do not keep as long as the sun-dried variety.
teardrop: small, yellow, pear-shaped tomatoes.

vietnamese mint has pungent, peppery, narrow leaves; also known as cambodian mint, pak pai and laksa leaf.

vinegar
balsamic: originally from Italy, there are now many balsamic vinegars on the market.
cider: made from apples.
red wine: based on fermented red wine.
white wine: made from white wine.

watercress one of the cress family, a large group of peppery greens.

witlof also known as chicory or belgian endive.

yogurt we used plain, unflavoured yogurt, unless otherwise specified.

zucchini also known as courgette.

conversion chart

MEASURES

One Australian metric measuring cup holds approximately 250ml, one Australian metric tablespoon holds 20ml, one Australian metric teaspoon holds 5ml.

The difference between one country's measuring cups and another's is within a 2- or 3-teaspoon variance, and will not affect your cooking results. North America, New Zealand and the United Kingdom use a 15ml tablespoon. All cup and spoon measurements are level. The most accurate way of measuring dry ingredients is to weigh them. When measuring liquids, use a clear glass or plastic jug with metric markings.

We use large eggs with an average weight of 60g.

DRY MEASURES

METRIC	IMPERIAL
15g	½oz
30g	1oz
60g	2oz
90g	3oz
125g	4oz (¼lb)
155g	5oz
185g	6oz
220g	7oz
250g	8oz (½lb)
280g	9oz
315g	10oz
345g	11oz
375g	12oz (¾lb)
410g	13oz
440g	14oz
470g	15oz
500g	16oz (1lb)
750g	24oz (1½lb)
1kg	32oz (2lb)

LIQUID MEASURES

METRIC	IMPERIAL
30ml	1 fluid oz
60ml	2 fluid oz
100ml	3 fluid oz
125ml	4 fluid oz
150ml	5 fluid oz (¼ pint/1 gill)
190ml	6 fluid oz
250ml	8 fluid oz
300ml	10 fluid oz (½ pint)
500ml	16 fluid oz
600ml	20 fluid oz (1 pint)
1000ml (1 litre)	1¾ pints

LENGTH MEASURES

METRIC	IMPERIAL
3mm	⅛in
6mm	¼in
1cm	½in
2cm	¾in
2.5cm	1in
5cm	2in
6cm	2½in
8cm	3in
10cm	4in
13cm	5in
15cm	6in
18cm	7in
20cm	8in
23cm	9in
25cm	10in
28cm	11in
30cm	12in (1ft)

OVEN TEMPERATURES

These oven temperatures are only a guide for conventional ovens. For fan-forced ovens, check the manufacturer's manual.

	°C (CELSIUS)	°F (FAHRENHEIT)	GAS MARK
Very slow	120	250	½
Slow	150	275 – 300	1 – 2
Moderately slow	160	325	3
Moderate	180	350 – 375	4 – 5
Moderately hot	200	400	6
Hot	220	425 – 450	7 – 8
Very hot	240	475	9

index

Are you missing some of the world's favourite cookbooks?

The Australian Women's Weekly cookbooks are available from bookshops, cookshops, supermarkets and other stores all over the world. You can also buy direct from the publisher, using the order form below.

MINI SERIES £3.50 190x138MM 64 PAGES

TITLE	QTY	TITLE	QTY	TITLE	QTY
4 Fast Ingredients		Gluten-free Cooking		Potatoes	
4 Kids to Cook		Grills & Barbecues		Quick Desserts	
15-minute Feasts		Healthy Everyday Food 4 Kids		Roast	
50 Fast Chicken Fillets		Ice-creams & Sorbets		Salads	
50 Fast Desserts		Indian Cooking		Simple Slices	
Barbecue Chicken		Italian Favourites		Simply Seafood	
Biscuits, Brownies & Bisottti		Indonesian Favourites		Soup plus	
Bites		Jams & Jellies		Spanish Favourites	
Bowl Food		Japanese Favourites		Stir-fries	
Burgers, Rösti & Fritters		Kebabs & Skewers		Stir-fry Favourites	
Cafe Cakes		Kids Party Food		Summer Salads	
Cafe Food		Lebanese Cooking		Tagines & Couscous	
Casseroles & Curries		Low-Fat Delicious		Tapas, Antipasto & Mezze	
Char-grills & Barbecues		Low Fat Fast		Tarts	
Cheesecakes, Pavlova & Trifles		Malaysian Favourites		Tex-Mex	
Chinese Favourites		Mince Favourites		Thai Favourites	
Chocolate Cakes		Microwave		The Fast Egg	
Crumbles & Bakes		Muffins		The Young Chef	
Cupcakes & Cookies		Noodles & Stir-fries		Vegetarian	
Dips & Dippers		Old-Fashioned Desserts		Vegie Main Meals	
Dried Fruit & Nuts		Outdoor Eating		Vietnamese Favourites	
Drinks		Packed Lunch		Wok	
Easy Pies & Pastries		Party Food			
Fast Fillets		Pickles and Chutneys			
Fishcakes & Crispybakes		Pasta		TOTAL COST £	

Photocopy and complete coupon below

Name _____

Address _____

_____ Postcode _____

Country _____ Phone (business hours) _____

Email*(optional) _____
By including your email address, you consent to receipt of any email regarding this magazine, and other emails which inform you of ACP's other publications, products, services and events, and to promote third party goods and services you may be interested in.

I enclose my cheque/money order for £ _____ or please charge £ _____
to my: ☐ Access ☐ Mastercard ☐ Visa ☐ Diners Club

Card number | | | | | | | | | | | | | | | |

3 digit security code *(found on reverse of card)* _____

Cardholder's
signature _____ Expiry date ____ / ____

To order: Mail or fax – photocopy or complete the order form above, and send your credit card details or cheque payable to: Australian Consolidated Press (UK), 10 Scirocco Close, Moulton Park Office Village, Northampton NN3 6AP, phone (+44) (01) 604 642200, fax (+44) (01) 604 642300, e-mail books@acpuk.com or order online at www.acpuk.com
Non-UK residents: We accept the credit cards listed on the coupon, or cheques, drafts or International Money Orders payable in sterling and drawn on a UK bank. Credit card charges are at the exchange rate current at the time of payment.
All pricing current at time of going to press and subject to change/availability.
Postage and packing UK: Add £1.00 per order plus 75p per book.
Postage and packing overseas: Add £2.00 per order plus £1.50 per book. **Offer ends 31.12.2008**